Table of Contents

So You've Retired - What's Next?

A Practical Guide For Your Happy Retirement

By
Olivia Greenwell

Disclaimer

© Copyright 2016 Olivia Greenwell

Dedication

I dedicate this book to you, my reader.

For I found daily inspiration while thinking of you and the adventures you are about to embark upon in this exciting new world of retirement.

I wish for you to fill your days with excitement, to realize your dreams and above all to find peace and serenity as you have never known before.

technicalities. You will find practical advice on what's important and what's not, and how to decide what works best for YOU.

I've got you covered when it comes to discovering what interests YOU, and will provide ideas to enhance your retirement years. Within these pages, you will find suggestions on a variety of topics, such as fun ways to travel, how to stay fit, methods to flex your mind, and learning to embrace what spirituality means to you. In addition to the suggestions provided, you'll find links and ideas for further research in the Resources at the end of the book. The options are as limited as your imagination!

This book is a comprehensive guide to assisting you on your quest to learn how to take advantage of your time and talents. My wish is that, as you pursue the peace and contentment of your retirement, I have played a small role in helping you discover what makes YOU happy, and how to enjoy your life to the fullest.

Chapter 1
So You're Retired

Congratulations! You've probably worked most of your life to reach the coveted milestone known as retirement, which, up to now, has always been a faint light at the end of a long tunnel. The passageway you've traveled has finally come to the end, and the previously dim goal has turned into a gloriously bright beacon, shining directly on YOU. Attaining this elusive moment will likely initiate celebrations of various proportions, gifts, tears, and cheers all around. The delight emanating from a new retiree has been known to inspire embarrassingly ridiculous happy dances (which you hope no one is quick enough to record on video and put online.) As joyous as this stage of life should be, it can also strike terror in the heart of the strongest warrior. At some point it's likely the idea will cross your mind that retirement implies you've been put out to pasture, and you have nothing to do for the next thirty-odd years.

To say that retirement is an adjustment is an understatement. Everything changes and your world may spin out of control if you don't come up with a plan for this new phase of your life. It doesn't require an outline for each moment of your day, as your previous employment might have dictated, but acknowledging the modifications your new life demands will allow you to make the most of your time, energy... and sanity!

Recognizing there will be alterations in your life is important. Anticipating and planning for changes will assist you in a successful transition. Keep a list of potential issues, especially those that pertain to your specific circumstances. Concerns can be addressed more efficiently when they are written down in black and white. You might consider beginning a journal, or a diary or a notebook to record your thoughts and ideas. (I'm not suggesting that you might be forgetful at this stage of your life. Ok, I *am* saying that. Make a list. Write things down.)

When you are suddenly available 24/7, you can spend more time with your family and friends. This is good. You've no doubt looked forward to having more free time and there are endless opportunities available to you and your loved ones. You might be the last of a group of friends to retire and they've been anxiously waiting for you to get involved in adventures you can all enjoy together. Your spouse might be thrilled to have you home and has her "honey-do" list ready for you to begin.

Newfound freedom has its downside too. Be cognizant of the fact that those around you might not have the luxury to come and go as easily as you, now that you are retired. Perhaps they don't have the funds to participate in your adventures, and they misinterpret your excitement as being boastful. Family and friends that aren't used to having you involved will need as much time to adjust as you do. Your spouse, not being used to having you around, might resent your constant presence at home. Recognize the potential of this happening in advance, and make a plan to avoid too much togetherness for a while. Communication is vital. Talk to your loved ones and discuss expectations about what will occur with your relationships when you retire.

Financial considerations are crucial for your retirement years. There is often a substantial reduction of income when a person leaves their job, and if they have not diligently saved their pennies over the years, they must adjust their new lifestyle to their retirement income, or lack thereof in some cases. Hopefully, you've made some preparation with an IRA, a pension plan, or other method to supplement your income and that will not be a worry for you. Life goes on, even on a limited budget and in subsequent chapters there will be ideas for enrichment and activities that don't cost a dime.

Perhaps you intend to work part-time, either at a job, or from your home. There are many "freelance" or self-employment opportunities to use your talents and interests to provide additional revenue. A few ideas are listed below.

- Pet sitting can be extremely lucrative and enjoyable if you like animals. You can provide this service in your home, preferably with a fenced yard. In some instances, you might be able to combine pet sitting and home sitting for people who like someone to occupy their home while they're away.
- Use your skills to freelance online. Clients seek assistance in hundreds of categories such

as writing projects, accounting, translation, photography, art, computer related jobs, and many other services. Freelance websites connect freelancers with clients, and they protect both parties.

- An experienced "handyman" can provide an economical option to people who just need a small job done and don't need a big contractor. Painting, cleaning and other minor jobs don't require many supplies, and your "elbow grease" can pay off handsomely.

- Gardening and landscaping opportunities are great for retirees who enjoy being outside and exercising their "green thumb." You might find there are people who are willing to pay for simply pulling weeds, so they can start their planting in clean soil.

- Check into becoming an Uber driver, if you enjoy driving and meeting new people.

- If you are physically able to keep up with a child, babysitting a few days a week can provide a nice income. Additionally, there are elderly folks who need assistance with cooking, cleaning, transportation or even a companion to read to them.

These are just a few ideas about ways to earn extra income without a huge commitment of time or resources. Don't forget to write a simple contract to confirm the terms of a job, and check your insurance policies to be sure you're covered for jobs in your home or vehicle.

The most significant aspect of retirement is the golden opportunity to focus on **what is most important at this stage of your life**. As we mature, learn life's lessons, and glean a wealth of experiences, we reach an understanding about what's essential to our physical, mental and spiritual well-being...and what's not. Retirement provides the chance to do the things we *want* to do, not the things we *have* to do. We've reached a point where we've earned the right to do whatever makes us happy. The goal of this book is to inspire people, provide useful information, and encourage retirees to discover avenues where they can enjoy their lives to the fullest. With awareness and a little preparation, you'll be ready to embark on this new journey. Welcome to the best time of your life!

Chapter 2
What's Next

You're officially retired and your opportunities are limitless! In truth, this realization could be a bit overwhelming and the adjustments daunting. Never fear! I'm here to present some ideas to help you transition from a working stiff to a life of leisure.

You're perfectly entitled to spend a week or two lolling about and literally doing nothing, if that makes you happy. After the dust settles and the excitement of celebrating your retirement wanes, it's a perfect opportunity to contemplate your situation and make some plans for the future.

The changes in a recently retired person's life will vary according to what they've been accustomed to doing. There will simply be more time to do the things they love! (And, if you aren't quite sure *what* you love, I'm going to help you find out.) If a person has always kept busy, the freedom to participate in their chosen activity will be a welcome respite. Golfers will enjoy more tee time. Shoppers will find exciting places to look for bargains. Hikers will seek out challenging trails. Pool loungers will have plenty of time to fine-tune their suntan.

An important step in paving the path toward a worry-free retirement is to take advantage of the freedom from obligations and get your house in order, both literally and figuratively. This is a perfect time to downsize. Clear away the clutter of unused possessions you've collected over a lifetime, and you'll sweep the cobwebs of disorganization out of your life. This gives you the pleasure of starting fresh, with nothing holding you back from moving forward.

Set a date and begin sorting through your home, attic, garage and storage areas. Depending on your hoarder status, this might take some time, but if you'll do a bit each day, it will soon be finished. You might be able to enlist help from your family and friends, if you entice them by saying it's a party (things are much easier after a few bottles of beer and some pizza). On a more serious note, this process will make life much easier, not only for YOU, but also for your family who will otherwise be forced to sort through your things after your death. Yea, you don't want that.

Here are the four areas you need to consider when organizing your belongings.

- **Throw away.** At one time, you might have thought you could *never* throw away your child's kindergarten scribbles, but now they're disintegrated and it's time to dispose of them. Most people only need to keep tax records/receipts for three years, so throw away those boxes from the past forty years. (You might need a shredder, or a big bon fire will work, especially if you're utilizing the party sham.) Items that are broken, melted, sticky, crumbling, rotted, greasy, mildewed, moth eaten, mice nibbled, unrecognizable, and/or beyond repair need to go in this pile. No, you can't fix it, and it will make some lovely flames.

- **Give away.** These items are not trash, but things you don't need or want. They might have a bit of redeeming value, but not enough to try to sell. Clothes that don't fit (or you haven't worn in ten years) are welcome contributions to thrift stores. Old towels and blankets are treasured by animal rescue organizations. Get plastic bins for items you want to pass along to your children, grandchildren or close friends. They might appreciate enjoying these things **now** rather than inheriting them after you pass on. Baby blankets (of now grown children), nick-knacks, Christmas decorations, artwork, tools, jewelry, and mementoes from family trips are just a few of the personal items you can pass on for others to enjoy. Sentimental items can be hard to part with, but knowing someone else will appreciate and value them will ease the pain.

- **Sell.** Items of value can be sold through a variety of methods, and with a bit of time and effort you'll accrue a nice fund for a vacation or other expenses. EBay is a popular choice for collectors' items and valuables. Designer clothes, handbags and shoes can be taken to a consignment store for the best price. Furniture, vehicles, musical instruments and large items are best advertised in a local newspaper or a "Thrifty Nickle" type magazine. Craigslist is widely used and often successful, but it has drawbacks so be cautious when posting and communicating! Household gadgets, kitchen do-dads, trinkets, books, toys and other small, inexpensive items sell quickly at yard sales and flea markets. Whatever does not sell, box it up and take it to a thrift store. Some charities offer free pick-up and you can schedule them to come at the end of your sale. Don't even think about saving it!

- **Keep.** Trust me; there will be plenty left over after you've gone through the previous three steps. If you take time to organize the stuff you've kept, it will help your life run much smoother. Put photos in albums or sort them into small boxes by the year they were taken. Heirloom quilts, tablecloths, and other cloth items should be stored in an airtight container. Display your mementos and souvenirs in a curio cabinet so that you can enjoy them, rather than have them stored in a box under your bed. (Yea, I know about the under-the-bed boxes. Things go in there and might not be found until twenty years later.) Organize your garage or tool shed where you can quickly locate what you need when you need it.

You will be surprised how much lighter (physically **and** emotionally) you will feel when you've accomplished clearing away unwanted things and putting the rest of your possessions in order. Now, there's one other significant issue of organization to address, and then you'll be free of my nagging and can move on to the fun stuff.

It's imperative that you review your important papers, make sure they are up to date, and placed in a location that your next of kin or designated representative can find them. Here is a list of the vital information others might need. You may not need an attorney to create some of these documents, however you must refer to your state's requirements to make certain they are written, signed and notarized in a legally binding manner.

- **Health Insurance Information.** If you become ill or incapacitated, someone should be able to locate your health insurance information and speak to health providers about your treatment.

- **Living Will.** In the event you are near death and unable to communicate, this document states your desires regarding extending extraordinary measures to keep you alive.
- **Power of Attorney.** This is a written authorization, giving your permission to allow another person to act on your behalf. You can make it as general or as specific as you want.
- **Will.** This document provides your direction in appointing someone to manage your estate and/or the distribution of your property after your death. If you do not wish for your will to be read before your death, make certain you provide the name of the attorney or law office that will have the will on file.
- **Directive for possessions not covered in a Will.** Most attorneys won't want to detail everything you own, and who you want to have it after your death. You can type a list, have it signed, notarized and added as an amendment to your will. It's also a good idea to discuss these wishes with your executor, or the person who will manage your estate.

- **Pets.** Your pet will be confused and lost without you if you reach a point that you can no longer care for them, for whatever reason. Arrange for a friend or family member to adopt your pet and provide a good home.
- **Funeral Arrangements.** Many people arrange their final wishes and, in some cases, pay for their funeral expenses in advance. This might include your selection of a casket and burial plot, or the process of cremation, if that is your preference. Leave this information where it can be promptly located.
- **Life Insurance.** Keep policies where your loved ones can find them and submit a claim. A recent report has shown that billions (yes, that's a B) of dollars of life insurance funds have been unclaimed because no one ever filed for them. They probably didn't even know there was a policy. If you have a life insurance policy, make sure your beneficiaries are able to collect the money you want them to have!

Many of these suggestions seem like common sense, but millions of people die without having a will or other directions to ease the burden of loved ones who are left to sort out the aftermath. Do yourself and your family a great favor by having these documents in order and easy to locate when needed.

Although the suggestions in this chapter might appear droll, they are important factors in your transition. Once your house and essential documents are in order, you will be able to enjoy the rest of your life without worrying about these issues. Now, let's move on to more exciting retirement ideas!

Chapter 3

Home Is Where The Heart Is

As you ease into the transition of your new lifestyle, consider if you are happy in your current home, or if the idea of relocating to another place appeals to you. If you are "getting your house in order" as discussed in the previous chapter, you might feel like you've gained confidence about making additional changes to create a worry-free retirement.

One or two people don't necessarily need a four-bedroom house with a huge yard, and the idea of a smaller home and garden (or no yard to mow!) might be just what you need. Moving is not fun, by any stretch of the imagination, but the benefits it could provide might be well worth the effort. Make an assessment of your current situation and consider the following questions.

- Is your house too big? Is it too small? Think of who will be living there, your specific needs, and if you can manage the basic upkeep.

- Is your current home in need of major repairs?
- Do you have the space for things you want, such as a garden, a pool or hot tub, or a fenced yard for pets?
- Do you anticipate the need for a home with easy access and wheelchair accommodations? Will you be able to maneuver stairs for the rest of your life?
- Are your family and friends within a reasonable distance?
- Do you like your neighbors and the neighborhood?
- Do you like the city, state, and country where you live? Is it safe? Is the cost of living reasonable? Do you like the climate?
- Would you consider moving to a foreign country? If not, perhaps a second vacation home is an option.
- Are there opportunities for the activities you love, such as parks, theater, sports events, restaurants, or beaches?
- Are there good hospitals and medical options available?

After reviewing this list, you might realize you're already in your perfect home! You are completely happy where you live and would never consider moving. Staying in an established location allows you to keep all the people you love, the places you enjoy, and the things you've grown accustomed to, and this is priceless! Perhaps there are some improvements, alterations, or redecorating you've wanted, but you've never had the time. Now that you're retired and had the opportunity to de-clutter, you can enjoy the rediscovered space in your home and make it look awesome. You can turn that extra bedroom into a workout room or a quiet reading area. You might want to add a patio, with a grill, and a hot tub! A new coat of paint in the kitchen, installing ceiling fans, or replacing carpet with wood flooring are projects that bring a fresh look to your home. The possibilities are endless! Even small changes will enhance the home you've lovingly built up over the years.

If your current living situation is not ideal, not "fixable," or you decide you just want to move and start fresh somewhere else, use the list above to help you decide what will work best for your specific needs, desires, and circumstances.

There's a new trend you might consider, which is most commonly referred to as "tiny houses". These very small homes are compact, efficient, and provide the obvious benefits of downsizing to the max. The economic tiny house can be built on a plot of land, or there are many that are constructed on a trailer base, allowing for moving to different locations. Tiny homes are certainly not for everyone, but they do appeal to many people and it might be an option to consider.

Another idea is to think about whether a retirement village would suit your needs. These communities vary in the options they offer. Some provide private homes or apartments for people who are self-sufficient, and some have transitional benefits that include caregivers and medical assistance for those who require help. Many of these retirement communities have amenities such as a clubhouse, pool, gym, transportation, cafeteria, and 24 hour security. Once again, this is not for everyone, but it could be an option to consider, especially if you are single and would appreciate the care and companionship these villages offer.

These are just a few suggestions to help you decide if you want to move, or if you *need* to move in order to create the lifestyle you desire. Sometimes it all boils down to what is most important to you, and that might not be 100 percent clear at this point in your life. Give it some thought, and don't be afraid to act if you decide on an option that will satisfy your needs and aspirations.

It's likely that you have grandchildren at this stage of your life, and spoiling them will occupy a lot of your newfound free time. Before you retired, you might not have been as close to your family as you would have liked. It's never too late to make up for the time lost. Talk to your family and let them know you want to spend time with them. It doesn't always have to be something magnanimous. Small things such as a walk in the park, or going to get ice cream can be more memorable than a big commitment, such as a week's vacation together. (A week? Yikes! Are we having fun yet?)

Often, the decision to be close to where your children and grandchildren live is a huge factor in relocating. Even if you don't currently live close to them, you can allot times throughout the year to visit them, go on adventures together, and enjoy the quality time you will spend with them. Seek activities that are age appropriate for the little ones. Schedule dates, as a group with the whole gang, and individually, one on one. This will reinforce the bond with your loved ones and provide some great memories!

Besides your family, another great joy of retirement is being able to spend more time with your friends. Now that you're free, you can plan adventures together! Cruises, road trips, or enjoying a favorite restaurant together is a great way to strengthen your friendships. You can open your home and invite people in, to enjoy a variety of activities such as dinner parties, game nights, watching a movie, book clubs, wine tasting, or simply provide a relaxing place to hang out.

You might find that you no longer have things in common with some friends. After you retire, you won't see your previous co-workers, clients, staff, and other people you were involved with on a daily basis. Time you spent working together with these associates, might have been the only mutual interest, despite the fact that you got along well. There could be a bit of jealousy or resentment that you're gone, off having fun, and they're still stuck at the job. If you have a truly good friend from work, this transition will not affect your relationship. For those that withdraw, don't take it personally. Even if you aren't close pals any longer, it's always nice to have acquaintances that you enjoyed for a season.

As you develop your interests, you will discover new friends that share your current retirement status, and/or the enjoyment of activities you have in common. For example, perhaps you've decided to volunteer at your public library. As you work with the staff and the patrons who frequent the library, you'll find people that share a mutual interest. Maybe you want to join a book club, or start one of your own. The love of reading brings people together in a cerebral way, and the casual atmosphere of a book club meeting lends itself to finding friends.

Many sports activities require team interaction, and being part of a group can be fun. If you're trying out a new venture, don't feel locked into it if it doesn't feel right. It's nice to try new things, but learn to trust your instinct about whether you should continue, or chalk it up as a learning experience and try something else. Friends often come along when you least suspect it, so don't feel forced to find new friends. Cherish the ones you have. Quality is always better than quantity.

As you move forward in your retirement, you will face many decisions. Some of them will be easy choices and others will be formidable. Weigh your options and go with your gut feeling. That always works best. Remember, home truly is where your heart is. You can't go wrong when you follow your heart!

Chapter 4
Embark on a New Adventure

Whether you have grand post-retirement plans, or you're just going with the flow and taking one day at a time, you are on the path of a new journey. If you don't have a specific strategy for what you want to do, just enjoy this new phase of your life until something strikes your fancy. Follow the advice of the popular expression - Don't worry. Be Happy.

The first three chapters of this book provided some guidance for recognizing the changes and the adjustments that will need to be made when you retire. Suggestions were given for adapting to your new life through "getting your house in order," making sure your important documents are up to date, and deciding where you want to live. Although certainly not mandatory, these ideas are intended to establish a firm foundation, to create an environment that is worry-free. Once this is accomplished and your "bases are covered," you will feel more confident about embarking on new adventures.

Many people have discovered that their newfound freedom allows time to travel and explore areas they couldn't before retirement. Travel expands the mind and makes you look at the world in a different way. Journey to unexplored areas of the US and foreign countries, learn more about other cultures, try unique foods, and bask in the awesome powerful feeling of going somewhere you've never been before. Make a list of the places, and transportation methods you enjoy, and don't be afraid to try new options. Here is a list of some travel options to consider.

- **Bicycle.** Discover parks, trails and other interesting routes. This simple, inexpensive transportation can be done alone, or with a group, and bike excursions can be as long or as brief as you like.

- **Motorcycle.** People who enjoy riding motorcycles can travel alone, or enjoy the comradery of a group, on a bike tour, or in a "poker run." As with bicycling, you can feel the wind in your hair for a few hours or several days.

- **Personal car, truck or SUV.** It's convenient

when you can drive your own vehicle and be able to proceed at your leisure. Road trips are infamous for the ability to stop to see unique sites along your way. They can produce memories that last a lifetime, although with small children, they can be challenging! (Are we there yet?) You could even consider buying a vintage car, which is not only fun to travel around in, but would qualify for joining a specialty vehicles owner's club. They offer opportunities for social meets, displaying unique cars, and other events centered on the common interest.

- **Tour Bus.** Many companies, both domestically and internationally, offer tours via bus. This method of travel can be slow, but it provides many benefits you wouldn't have on faster transport. You'll have the ability to see the scenery that you would miss on an airplane, plus the friendly atmosphere of being with a group of like-minded people. Often led by a seasoned tour guide, bus tours are great for single travelers too, because they are instantly part of a team.

- **Train.** Trains are fun and you can enjoy the passing scenery at a faster pace than a bus or personal vehicle. Unfortunately, train routes in the US are somewhat limited, but in Europe and other countries, this is an excellent mode of transportation. For the ultimate in luxury you could take a trip on the legendary Orient Express, with luxurious sleeper cabins and fine dining.

- **Recreational Vehicle.** Many retirees love the idea of traveling in an RV. They have the freedom to go where they want, when they want, and without concern for hotel reservations or restaurant stops. The camping experience is memorable as you meet other travelers on the same wave length. Often RVs are a means to live in another area for a period of time, such as "snowbirds" who like to reside in a warmer climate during winter.

- **Airplane.** This is obviously the fastest mode of transportation if you only want to get from point A to point B. When making reservations, find flights that allow lots of time between multiple legs, and enjoy the variety of the different airports along your journey.

- **Cruise Ship.** An adventure on a cruise ship provides transportation to a destination (often multiple ports) but it also provides almost everything else you need for a trip – a place to sleep, food, entertainment, scenery, and plenty of people to meet. An "all-inclusive" cruise is relatively worry-free and reasonably priced, when you consider what you get for the fare. There are actually people who have chosen to make a cruise ship their retirement home. They travel year round, with all their requirements met, often for a cost cheaper than other retirement options!

Contemplate some ideas about where you'd like to go, and what you'd like to see and experience. Often your destination will dictate the means of travel that best suits the journey. For instance, if you want to visit the Grand Canyon, a personal vehicle, RV, or tour bus would be the best options for viewing various locations around this huge tourist site. You can get to Bermuda by plane, but a cruise ship will casually take you there and allow plenty of time for you to explore the island. A visit to the United Kingdom would require a flight from the US, but after you arrive, you will have many travel options, including the underground "tube" when you're in London. (Mind the Gap!)

As you plan your adventures, you can solicit the help of a travel agent who will offer advice on many issues. Virgin travelers or people uncomfortable making their own plans should seek the assistance of a travel agency. (There is usually no charge to the consumer, because the agents are paid by the company to book reservations.)

Don't forget that you will need a passport for traveling outside the US. For first time applicants this can take up to six weeks so plan accordingly! Watch the expiration date of a current passport and start the renewal process when it's six months from being expired. Additionally, a travel visa and/or immunizations are required to enter some countries. Research your destination before you make reservations to ensure a smooth adventure. As of 2016, cruise ships **disembarking and returning** to a US port do not require a passport. A birth certificate is acceptable. However, if you are visiting a foreign country during the cruise and need to depart in the event of an emergency, you will have difficulties trying to exit the country via airplane without a passport. It's simply a good idea to have a valid passport!

If you are a single traveler, without a spouse or travel companion, there are great options for tours with a group, who will embrace a solo tourist. If "double occupancy" is required, tour group representatives can help match you with another single traveler. Some cruise ships offer rooms for single occupants, including a lounge area to encourage the solo travelers to mingle!

Many people enjoy planning their own trips. They search the internet for information about destinations, reservations, car rentals, cruises, and just about anything you can imagine regarding traveling. **Always** check for "senior" discounts and last minute deals. (One of the benefits of being retired is the freedom to take advantage of situations like a half-price cruise that leaves in one week.) Some cruise lines offer a price guarantee, and they will match a lower price found on another website. However, some of these offers require certain stipulations, so read the fine print. Always read the fine print!

Don't think that some of the adventures I've suggested have to be long, expensive or complicated. Take a mid-week break and drive a few hours to an area you love and spend one night in an inexpensive hotel. (Many hotels and attractions have lower prices Monday – Thursday.) Take an afternoon to enjoy a museum or science center. Join your grandchildren in the park for a bike ride and picnic. Here's a fun fact: The US National Park Service offers US citizens or permanent residents age 62 and over a **lifetime** Senior Pass for a one-time cost of $10. Previously known as the Golden Age Passport, the pass admits the senior and the passengers in the vehicle! How's that for a freebie!

Envision the things that you love, the things that bring you joy, and the things you always wanted to do. Some people find it helps to brainstorm and make a list of possibilities, to get their thoughts written down for later review. Develop a hobby or activity that you already know you enjoy, but that you previously didn't have time to indulge. Do some investigating and see what it takes to accomplish a dream you've had. Perhaps you always felt artistic. Take a painting, photography or writing class and see if it sparks more interest, or if you can put it behind you without any desire to continue. Learn a new language or how to play a musical instrument, talk to your friends and family about their interests and get together for activities you can enjoy as a group.

The adventure possibilities are virtually endless. It all depends on what you want to do. Don't feel like you have to be doing something fantastic every minute of the day, but make plans to have a bit of fun several times each week. You might think that some of these options are beyond your budget, but you will find most of them very economical. By putting away a few dollars here and there, you'll soon be on your way to an exciting adventure!

Chapter 5

Eat to Live ~ Live to Eat

As you venture into your retirement years, maintaining a healthy body is imperative! You need to be in good physical condition in order to do all the things you want to do. Excess weight and being out of shape can prevent you from enjoying your life to the fullest.

It can be challenging to change a lifetime of poor eating habits and a sedentary existence. Perhaps your pre-retirement job kept you deskbound, or your lunch consisted of a soda and a bag of M & M's. Maybe swinging by the coffee shop for caffeine and do-nuts on your way to work was an essential part of your morning routine. Many work settings indulge in social activities such as potluck meals, birthday parties, and after-work visits to a sports bar for munchies and adult beverages. Ok, it was fun, but in many instances, there might have been a sense of duty to participate. Now that you're retired, you can leave those obligations behind you. This is the perfect opportunity to make a reckoning of unhealthy behaviors, and strive toward better choices.

Diet is a four-letter word, and I mean that in the nastiest sort of way. Just the mention of the word sends fear and loathing into the boldest humans. Diets are not fun, they are restrictive and tortuous, and nobody wants to be around folks who are dieting. When people go on a diet, they turn into grouchy, pathetic zombies, stumbling around in a food-induced craze. Trust me. I speak from experience as a dieter and as a spectator of others dieting attempts. I think I can safely say that nobody likes a diet.

That being said (and made explicitly clear) eating healthy food and learning to control portions will help you lose weight and make you feel better. If you need some help recognizing accurate portions, check out the "portion plate" and other convenient measuring devices that make it easy to determine the correct serving size. Simply avoiding usage of the "d" word will work wonders on your attitude and help you make changes to your eating habits without feeling deprived. Think about managing what you eat from an optimistic view, rather than the negativity a strict diet often elicits.

Most adults recognize foods that are good for you and those that are not so good. I won't even describe them as "bad" because the idea behind what I suggest is that even foods that are considered evil can be eaten in moderation. Take time to become informed about the truth in food production, labeling, and frequent false or misleading information. A good example of this is the butter vs. margarine argument. Butter is high in cholesterol, saturated fat and calories and yet it's a natural food made from real milk. Margarine is an artificial "spread" that is made from vegetable oil and often contains trans fat (the bad kind). Studies have shown that margarine increases heart disease risk, while butter may be nonthreatening. And yet, the use of butter is considered "bad" and the use of margarine is acceptable. It's important to do your homework and research the foods that you love and learn the truth about whether they are harmful, or healthy in moderation.

If you are insecure about your understanding of food, seek information online or take a nutrition class to help you become more confident. Some health insurance policies cover nutrition counseling, and free information can be obtained at your local library and health department. It's important to view your new eating decisions in a fun, optimistic fashion. Look at it as another adventure - an opportunity to learn, and even make new friends in a cooking class or at the farmer's market checking out the fresh veggies.

Many restaurants offer "heart healthy" options so you can still enjoy eating out with your friends and family. A salad is always a good choice but keep in mind that "low-fat" salad dressings often have four times the calories of regular dressing. If you haven't eaten at a favorite place in years and you just can't resist the hot wings, fettuccini alfredo, or that yummy dessert, then go for it! Splurging occasionally isn't the end of the world. Divide large servings in half and take some home for lunch the next day. If you are on a cruise, resisting many of the exciting menu items can be impossible. A saint could not fight the urge to try the chocolate molten cake, and I'm not even going to pretend it's healthy.

Take advantage of senior discounts offered at many restaurants and fast food locations. Many places don't advertise their discount so be sure to ask! Don't be hesitant to use a 2-for-1 coupon, or arrive before the crowds for an "early bird" special. When eating at a buffet, take small portions of what you really want, and only go back if you are truly hungry. It's tempting to feel like you need to get your money's worth, but consider how much better you'll feel walking away satisfied and not stuffed.

Sharing food is a primal activity. It's an opportunity to expand your senses, and share your home and your table with friends and family. Visit a vineyard and participate in wine tastings. Enjoy themed dinner parties, neighborhood bonfires where you'll eat hotdogs and s'mores, and church potlucks. Cook with your grandchildren and don't be afraid to get messy. Volunteer at a soup kitchen, not only to "give back" but also to help you realize and appreciate what you have in your life.

You must "eat to live." The choice of what you eat, how you approach the idea of being healthy, and the joy that can come from eating and sharing food and drink with others is powerful. It's a basic function of life but it can be an extraordinary delight. "Live to eat" doesn't mean you become a glutton. It means you finally realize there can be joy in experimenting with new tastes, flavors and different ways to enjoy food. You don't have to eat huge amounts to appreciate the dish.

There is no firm answer to each person's situation. If you have **any** medical issues you should **always** consult with your physician before making changes to what you eat. Individual health conditions, prescription drugs and other factors might prevent you from the ideas I've suggested. Perhaps the best advice I can give is, simply be aware of your eating habits and aim toward making them as healthy as possible.

Chapter 6
Exercise and Stay Fit

Part of being healthy is making good choices about the foods you eat. An equally important aspect of getting and staying fit is to remain active. Becoming a couch potato might have been on your retirement to-do list, but after a few weeks I'm certain you're ready to check that off and move on. So now, if your muscles aren't withered from inactivity, get off the couch and do something!

At the beginning of each year, fitness gyms are swarming with people who've made a New Year's resolution to get in shape. By February, the crowds have disappeared and only a few faithful remain. Let me be clear. There is nothing wrong with going to a gym! Contrary to my aversion to regimented diets, gyms, hospital sponsored fitness centers and organizations like the YMCA offer some great benefits. Just make sure your attraction to a gym is realistic and you're sure about it before making a long-term commitment.

Fitness establishments provide more exercise equipment than anyone could want and fitness instructors to help you figure out how to operate the complicated machines. Many places offer classes in a variety of areas such as nutrition instruction, yoga, spin racing, weight lifting, and programs like Zumba, kickboxing and self-defense. Some fitness establishments have a swimming pool for water aerobics, lessons and even free swim periods. A few fitness centers include luxury options such as saunas, steam rooms, tanning beds, juice bars, personal trainers, and massage services!

Joining a gym or other fitness program can be a great way to get started, or to continue staying in good physical condition. It feels nice to treat yourself to this specialized service, and to have access to professional equipment and knowledgeable instructors. The group atmosphere can be encouraging as you see others working toward similar goals. Some people might find themselves intimidated by other people, you know, those slim, tan, beautiful, muscular ones that barely break a sweat. Thankfully, "no judgement" policies are gaining popularity among gyms to discourage the idea of comparing yourself to   others.

A negative aspect of a gym or fitness center is the cost. Some establishments require a membership fee or a long-term commitment, which they usually want paid in full before you even begin. What happens if you don't like it? Check the refund policy before you sign a contract! Many gyms charge extra for personal instruction, specific classes and those luxury services. There are reasonably priced gym services that are basic, if you don't care about all the "bells and whistles." Check with your local gym to see if they offer a tiered pricing structure, where it's less expensive to go at off-peak hours, which is perfect for a retiree's flexible schedule! It's up to each person to make the decision if the benefits of going to a gym supersede the cost.

Another consideration about joining a gym is that you have to get up and GO to the gym. Yea, bummer. It's amazing how easy it is to talk yourself out of dressing in your workout gear, with the burning question - do I shower before so I'll look good, knowing I'm going to get sweaty and need to shower after? Then, you have to get in your car and drive to the gym in the heat, wind, rain, snow or whatever the weather decides to be that day. Of course, I'm being factious. The point I'm trying to make is that going to a gym has its advantages, but don't overlook the downside. There are a variety of other activities that you can do beyond gym life, and most of them don't cost money!

Walking is probably one of the best exercises you can do at your own convenience, and it's free! Use your phone or other listening device to enjoy music while you walk, but always be aware of your surroundings to be safe. Check your phone for apps that will help you keep track of your progress, provide maps for routes to explore, and even monitor your heart rate. Many people prefer to walk in quiet, and meditate, pray or think about their day. Follow a route around your neighborhood, walk in a park, on the beach, or use a local school's football field track. (FYI – four times around equals one mile.) Many communities have mile markers on bridges, scenic routes and even inside shopping malls. If you want to walk in the woods or other isolated area, find a buddy to join you. For safety's sake, if you walk alone, take a walking stick, whistle, pepper-spray (for wild animals/crazy people), a cell phone and plenty of water in case you lose your way. Brisk walking is refreshing and it gives you a chance to enjoy nature and clear your mind.

Many people who enjoy walking will move on to jogging and maybe even train to run a marathon. For some, a marathon is a possibility to consider and an admirable accomplishment for those who train and become successful participants. Plus, there are some really cool medals that you get, along with the bragging rights that you actually ran a marathon! If a full marathon (approximately 42k/26 miles) is too big a leap, you could try a 5k, 10k or a half-marathon. There are races that offer fun elements such as bubbles, rainbow colors, hot chocolate, rock 'n roll, and even marathons for Disney lovers. The American Heart Association and other organizations have events that raise money for worthwhile causes through walks and runs. Check online to discover endless opportunities for events that match your interests, and will provide fun while helping you stay fit!

Golfers around the world would be furious if I didn't recommend their sport as a great form of exercise, and it is. Golf provides a day out in nature, being active, and a chance to be with friends who also enjoy the sport. The same can be said for tennis, community baseball and basketball teams, swimming, skating, volleyball, croquet, or just about any activity you have fun doing. Don't feel like you always have to be with a group of other seniors. Being around young people helps keep us on our toes, and we might even learn something from the whippersnappers!

If you'd like to combine staying fit with doing a good deed, consider volunteering at a hospital, museum, an animal shelter, or other prospects that interest you. You'll stay busy walking and running errands, and get to be around people of like minds. If you enjoy animals, there is always a need for people to walk, bathe and even foster a pet until it finds its forever home. Owning your own pet can be a great experience too! You might find you want to get involved in professional dog shows, either as a participant or as a spectator. Even if your pet is a Heinz 57 mutt, you'll enjoy the companionship of your furry friend, and daily walks will be good for both of you.

Geocaching is an increasingly popular activity for people of all ages. It's a modern day game of hide-and-seek, using GPS and navigational methods to locate hidden treasures. Many people join geocaching clubs and participate in team searches. It's a great activity to get some exercise, enjoy nature and utilize your sleuthing skills.

If dancing tickles your fancy, take lessons and learn to trip the light fantastic. There are numerous options depending on what interests you and a companion, if you want to learn as a couple. Ballroom dancing is always popular, as is square dancing and country style line dancing. In addition to the great exercise it provides, learning to belly dance or hula dance allows you to embrace and appreciate a different culture. If you're a little shy or concerned about what your two left feet will do, buy or rent an instructional DVD and learn the basics at home.

There are many opportunities within your daily routine to help you stay fit. When you go get your mail, walk around the block. Do some sit-ups while you're watching TV. Always take stairs in lieu of an elevator. Stretch your muscles while you're cooking. It's not rocket science - just move your booty whenever you have a minute or two.

DVDs and videos on YouTube are a great way to explore endless possibilities for exercise and enrichment without much investment. The benefit of viewing them in the privacy of your living room allows you to discover what truly interests you. Don't be afraid to step out of your comfort zone and try something new. You can always say you tried it, and it wasn't your cup of tea. Think about some of these suggestions and brainstorm for some of your own ideas as you seek your niche in the world of staying in shape. As always, do the things you like and the things that bring you joy. You'll feel better, look better and be more content with your life when you stay fit!

Chapter 7
Flex Your Mind

It's important to keep your body in shape and it's equally vital to exercise your mind. Seek activities that will expand your knowledge and have fun at the same time. Despite the advice of a well-known adage, you **can** teach an old dog new tricks, and learning new things will magnify your world!

Reading is a wonderful opportunity to explore new ideas, and whether you prefer fiction or non-fiction, you can drift off into an adventure in your mind. Reach outside your normal reading preferences and learn about things that aren't familiar, to stretch your imagination. Most communities have wonderful libraries where you can find a plethora of options besides books. Some libraries might charge a small fee for a membership, but most have no charge, unless you keep loaned items over the due date.

At your library, you will often discover free classes or lectures on a variety of subjects, along with computers, eBooks, books on CD, movies, and music videos and CDs. Log in to your library online and search the library's selection, put items on hold, and renew checkouts. If you want something that is not available at your local library, they have access to an interlibrary loan service, which can get an item from another system. Volunteering at a library is a great way to help the staff, promote the activities, assist with used book sales, and get to know likeminded folks.

Additional ideas to keep your mind active are brainteasers like crosswords, word search puzzles, and Sudoku, which can be played by yourself. Board games such as chess, backgammon, Scrabble, Monopoly, picture puzzles, and a horde of other offerings will provide challenges as well as fun. Many games involve team players and test your skills in drawing (Pictionary), trivia (Trivial Pursuit), strategy (Apples to Apples), coordination (Twister), and brain skills (Cranium.) There are the "luck of the dice" games like Sorry, and Candy Land, which you can enjoy with your young grandchildren. Card tournaments that include Bridge, Pinochle, Hearts and Poker encourage competition, team play and even a bit of gambling, if you desire. Whether you like silly party games, seriously competitive choices or children's games, don't be afraid to branch out and learn some up-to-date alternatives. Although playing these games in "real life" allows you to be involved with other people in a social setting, many are also available to play on your phone, iPad or computer.

You might be in a situation that you'd like to continue your education, either toward a degree or simply for personal enrichment. Inquire at your local college, trade school or university, as many provide tuition-free classes to seniors. Community colleges and civil organizations provide free or low cost classes on many subjects. For courses that involve making an item, such as art projects, sewing, or gardening, there will probably be a fee for materials. You can learn a foreign language (from beginner to advanced), home decorating, creative writing, computer programs, and many other stimulating choices.

Many businesses offer free lessons in their stores, to help customers learn a new craft, and of course buy the supplies from them! Fabric stores, sewing centers and craft suppliers offer a variety of learning experiences, such as floral arrangement, children's crafts and picture framing. Home building stores have free classes on such topics as how to install wood flooring, caulk a bathtub, and other home improvements. Garden centers and nurseries will offer advice on the best plants to grow in the region where you live. Think of the different ways you can learn more about a subject that interests you, and you'll most likely find a class to help you learn more about it.

You might be in a situation that you are an expert in a skill and would like to offer your services to teach a class, or mentor a person in need of your expertise and knowledge. If you enjoy working with children, you might consider being a tutor at a local public school. Libraries, schools, hospitals and daycare centers appreciate volunteers who will come and simply read to children. Some people, whose first language is not English, need a person to help them learn to read, write and speak their new language. This would be an extremely rewarding opportunity for retirees looking for a way to make a difference in their community.

In discussing methods to keep your mind active, I would be remiss in not addressing the issue of

Alzheimer's disease. There are ongoing advances in diagnosing and finding a cure for this debilitating illness. Exercising the mind through brain strengthening activities has not been a proven remedy against the disease, but it certainly can't hurt. Inspiring stories, such as that of recording artist Glen Campbell, indicate that the effects of Alzheimer's can be delayed. With assistance from his family, Glen was able to continue to tour and perform years longer than expected. Simply knowing that you should do everything you can to keep your mind strong is reason enough to flex your brain on a daily basis.

Chapter 8
Take Advantage of Technology

Learning to keep up with the latest information about computers and mobile phones can be daunting for those who are "technology challenged." We love our comfort zone, and often the newfangled gadgets don't make sense to us older folks. You must take into account that it was just over twenty years ago that cellular phones became widely used. I barely had my flip phone figured out and along comes the iPhone, android phone, and other James Bond devices I can't even comprehend. When my flip phone died last year, I went to my cell service store and, at the badgering of my adult children, purchased an iPhone. I asked the representative for an instruction book and she looked at me as if I had two heads, and finally told me I can find out how to operate it online. Right. So, I did what every self-respecting, technology ignoramus does and asked my grandchildren.

I am among many that don't really care about the most up to date apps and social network opportunities. I know people who still have a landline phone, and refuse to get a cell phone, so I consider myself in the middle of the dilemma. However, I recognize that there are many people who **love** to learn the newest technology. I bow to their fearlessness. The same can be said for the computer wizards, who understand how to use a computer to its maximum potential. When I learn a new program or how to post photos on Facebook I pull a muscle patting myself on the back. I've discovered a whole world of knowledge and opportunities. If I can do it, anyone can!

For those feeling technically adventurous there are free resources available online where you can learn to code in many different programming languages. It can be quite fun and challenging to create programs to advance your reach into the cyber world. You can construct your own webpage, blog, app or other online site, and manage it all by yourself, if you're so inclined.

The ironic issue about learning how to do things on a computer is that you can find out how **on your computer.** YouTube has endless tutorials on everything from **A**pple to **Z**programs. You can get in-depth instruction and learn how to do just about anything online, from fixing a leaky toilet to braiding hair. It's overwhelming, but in a good way. The opportunities are virtually endless.   Just find something you're interested in and charge ahead!

Computers and smart phones are a great means to stay up to date on local events, festivals, concerts, fundraisers, the weather, and your grandchildren's school activities. Facebook, Twitter, facetime, and other social networks allow people to stay in touch with family and friends. Sites such as LinkedIn provide a platform for professionals to network. A multitude of dating sites guarantee to find your "perfect match." I should mention, from personal experience, their promise is dubious and don't believe everything that people write on their profiles. More importantly for online daters, be safe by always meeting for the first time in a public area, and let a friend know where you're going!

Banking and bill paying is a breeze when you use the online sites. Most businesses offer the option of "going paperless" which speeds the billing and payments along and helps the environment. As convenient as it is to access so many ventures online, it's important to always be alert for frauds, cons, and fake emails that implore you to reply with confidential information. Never follow a link within an email instructing you to amend your banking details, or provide your personal password. These messages are frighteningly realistic, but banks would NEVER ask you for this information so call them rather than respond to the email. When paying for an online purchase with a credit card always confirm the site address is secure. HTTP stands for "Hyper Text Transfer Protocol", and is used in the URL address for browsing websites that have no login or need to be secure. HTTP**S** includes **SSL** - Secure Sockets Layer, which uses encryption to keep financial data, passwords, or any sensitive information safe and secure. In addition to these cautions, it's vital to keep the security and anti-virus programs on your computer up to date, to avoid infection. Change passwords often and don't use "password" as your password. Seriously, millions of people do this!

When planning a trip you can explore endless adventures, and search for the best values on transportation, lodging and excursions. Decide in advance what you really want to do, and don't waste your time on "tourist traps" or things that don't interest you. Travel websites such as AAA, Lonely Planet and Rick Steves are valuable tools to find information about tourist sites, hotels and restaurants. Some sites like TripAdvisor have the added bonus of unbiased reviews from travelers who've been there. Unconventional travelers might enjoy the economic option of Airbnb, where you find unique lodging situations in over 190 countries. If a cruise is on your horizon, after you book a voyage, you can join a chat room of people going on the same trip. You will find great suggestions from seasoned cruisers, and the option to make plans to meet for drinks and group activities when you get onboard.

Look for local activities that you can join in. Car club activities, dog shows, beach cleanup days, art festivals, and city sponsored events that provide entertainment and great food. Some cities encourage the film industry to come to their town and shoot movies or music videos. The producers will advertise for "extras" for background and crowd scenes, and sometimes they even pay for a day's work. Wouldn't it be fun to brag about being in a movie?!

Perhaps you have an issue that is close to your heart and you want to start an online Blog, to offer advice and discuss the interest with other people on the same wavelength. Maybe you have a product or service you'd like to sell, and you can start your own website to advertise the items. Swap sites and resale opportunities are there for practically all interests. Maybe you'd like to sell some items on EBay and that could turn into a full time venture!

Even if you don't "surf the internet" on a daily basis, the computer is a valuable tool for keeping up with your photos, documents and correspondence. You can finally write that book that's been on your to-do list forever! Many people of retirement age want to write their memoirs, or their life experiences to share with their family. They don't care about being published but that might be an option too!

These suggestions for keeping your mind active are simply the tip of the iceberg. There are so many opportunities to expand your mind and keep it flexed. Whether you're a seasoned tech wiz, or a newbie, learn to utilize the gifts of the wonderful technology that's available. It's all there at the tip of your typing fingers!

Chapter 9
Embrace Your Spirituality

More than at any other point in our lives, in our retirement we contemplate our mortality and increasingly consider our spirituality. We ask ourselves those vexing questions - *Why are we here? - Where did we all come from? - Is there something bigger than us out there? - What is my purpose in life?* We want to resolve our minds with our thoughts on the answers, and find peace.

It used to be common for a person to be "born, raised and die" in one specific religious denomination. Traditions run deep in many families and there is nothing wrong with having firmly held beliefs that continue through a person's entire life. There is comfort in familiarity and peace in embracing an ancestor's religion.

Being a member of a congregation means you are part of a family of like-minded people. It's a place where you feel comfortable and can find harmony as you interact with others. There may be extra offerings beyond the walls of your church where you can participate in sports teams, and other community events. Churches often have groups that meet specifically for the needs of single members, seniors, or mothers who need a day off.

If you are a member of a religious community, use your retirement freedom to become more involved in your church, synagogue or house of worship. There are many opportunities for "lay persons" who want to contribute to the welfare of their congregation. Discuss your desire with your pastor or church leader to match your skills with needed tasks. Perhaps you have a lovely garden, and would like to provide some flower arrangements to enhance the church, or you enjoy teaching and would like to assist in a Sunday school class or bible study. If your talents involve organization, you can help plan a craft bazar, Christmas program, food pantry for the needy, fundraiser, or any church event that needs help. Volunteer opportunities are vast within the church community, and your contribution will always be appreciated.

As people get older, they might find that their beliefs and views have changed over the years, and an organized religion no longer suits their needs. They might have discovered that they can no longer support the strict doctrine or the demands required to maintain a membership in a church. As our world expands, we embrace the issues that are important to us. If those issues include religious dogma, such as forbidding women in the priesthood, birth control, LGBT rights, or other social situations that are in conflict with your beliefs, it's probably time to make a change. When people reach this stage, they could be drawn into a different religion that meets their current needs, or they could decide not to be involved in any organized belief system. For many, leaving a religion they've been a part of for most of their life is difficult. If possible, maintain friendships. If that's not feasible, you have to do what you believe is right.

The bottom line in determining where you stand regarding being involved in an organized religion, or choosing to move in another direction, is to **follow your heart**. As we get older (and so much wiser!), we know what we want and what we don't want. We're "over the hill" and we want our time to be spent in happiness and contentment. Coming into retirement is reason enough to evaluate our spiritual needs and make changes when we feel that's the best direction.

Just because a person leaves a religious organization doesn't mean they've become a bad person. Individuals will maintain their core beliefs, morals, ethics and values regardless of whether they go to church or not. In fact, breaking away from the constraints of a religion can produce a personal spiritual awakening. You are free to choose whatever you want to believe!

Once you are permitted to open your mind and your heart, there is a bounty of spiritual enrichment you can embrace. For instance, if you consider yourself a "Christian" perhaps you always felt a bit guilty or hesitant to accept some of the teachings of Buddhism or Taoism, or belief in other deities, like the Hindu god Ganesha, who creates the faith to remove obstacles. In retirement, there's time to research and delve into different religious teachings, to learn and make up your own mind about what you really believe. Without religious affiliation, you are now open to appreciate the lessons that speak to you, regardless of the source.

Nature is one of the most powerful ways to worship. "If you wish to know the divine, feel the wind on your face and the warm sun on your hand"(Buddha). A glorious sunrise or sunset, the view from a magnificent mountain, the ocean's waves, and the fragrance of a beautiful flower are all forms of adoration and thanks to a higher power, whoever that might be to you. Sit in the stillness of a garden, or beneath the roar of a waterfall and experience a spiritual high that you might not have ever had before. Take a hike in the forest, watch the flow of a river, witness birds and other animals in the wild. Enjoy a picnic in a scenic setting, or find a deserted area to lie on a blanket and look at the stars at night. The possibilities to gain inspiration and spiritual fulfillment from nature's bounty are endless.

Music is a spectacular way to bring joy into your life. There are times when the hard beat of a rock song keeps you moving and dancing. At other times, the music from a symphony might bring tears to your eyes, and fill you with peace. Music is so diverse, and it can produce a variety of emotions that will meet a spiritual need in your life. Take advantage of any opportunity to expand your musical preferences, such as going to an opera or a jazz performance. If you're so inclined, learn to play a musical instrument that you've always enjoyed. Music offers so many benefits and there is something for everyone to enjoy!

Spirituality can be found in the simplest things in life. The giggle of a baby, the sweet cuddle of a puppy, and the love of a good friend are events that bring a smile to our face and lightness to our soul. Embrace everything that happens in your daily life. When we were young, we didn't always have time to stop and smell the roses. Do it now! It's never too late to start appreciating all the good things this world has to offer.

A great method to have that "feel good" attitude is by looking for ways to give back, to return some of your joy to others. Find avenues to volunteer your time and talents. Depending on your skills, you might be able to join a team of charitable workers on an overseas mission, or help with a local homeless shelter. The "pay it forward" concept offers the chance to payback someone's kindness to you by being kind to someone else. Perhaps the driver ahead of you paid your fee on a toll road. You can't pay that person back, but you can pay it forward. The next time you have the opportunity, pay the toll for the driver behind you. It doesn't have to involve money and can be something as simple as helping someone with a problem, remembering how someone once helped you.

A similar idea is a "random act of kindness." Look for chance encounters that will give you the opening to do something nice, without any forethought. Say hello to a person who looks sad, buy a soda for a teenager, pick a flower and hand it to the next person you see. There are limitless ways you can show kindness when you're aware and looking for ways to spread joy. And, it's ironic that when you show kindness to others, you are rewarded by the happiness it brings!

Regardless of whether you are actively involved in a religious organization or you haven't stepped foot in a church in 50 years, there are countless means to bring a sense of worship, reverence and spirituality into your daily life. Take delight in spending time with your friends and family, enmesh yourself in nature, bask in the places you love to visit, dance to the music that makes you happy, and cloak yourself in the peace of embracing your own spirituality. There's no magic formula. It's simply what brings joy to your heart and contentment to your soul.

Chapter 10
Your Very Own Bucket List

Although the term "bucket list" was used before the movie of the same name, it became a well-known maxim after the story of two terminally ill friends decided to make a wish list of things they wanted to do before they "kicked the bucket." Viewers embraced the idea of fulfilling lifelong dreams and daring adventures when they had nothing left to lose. Here are a few items on the bucket list that these characters created.

- Witness something truly majestic
- Laugh until I cry
- Drive a Shelby Mustang
- Kiss the most beautiful girl in the world
- Get a tattoo
- Skydiving
- Spend a week at the Louvre
- See the pyramids

Everyone has something you've always wanted to do. Maybe you never had time, money, opportunity, or the courage to accomplish the fantasy. As with the above example, a wish list of things you'd like to do doesn't necessarily have to be expensive or a huge investment of your time. And, your list of challenges doesn't have to wait until you are on death's doorstep. It is simply what YOU want to do at this stage of your life.

I have a friend, who in her mid-40's, found herself at a crossroad in her life. In order to remain optimistic about her future, the idea was presented to her that she was in a position to do anything she wanted with her life. She was encouraged to think "outside the box" and imagine something she'd always dreamed of doing, but up to this point in her life circumstances had prohibited. She was free to do whatever her heart desired, and she began to brainstorm the possibilities. During several memorable vacations to Disney World, she recalled saying how much fun it would be to work there. It was a silly daydream, but the more she thought about it, the more she liked the idea. She decided it wouldn't hurt to check it out. A few weeks later, and after some basic inquiries, she was in Lake Buena Vista, Florida at the Disney World Casting Center. After an interview, was offered a role, and two weeks later she moved into an apartment near the Magic Kingdom to begin her fantasy, which lasted over ten years.

Of course, the situation I've described was a long-term experience, and a life-changing event. Not everyone is in a position to make such a drastic transformation, nor does everyone want to alter his or her entire future based on a daydream. It's simply an example of a person with an opportunity, who took a chance. It provided her with a sense of adventure and incredible happiness. By the way, when my friend left Disney World, she became a flight attendant, which was another dream on her wish list. "You are never too old to set another goal, or to dream a new dream" (C.S. Lewis).

When you get ready to make your very own bucket list, brainstorm to consider **anything and everything** that sounds intriguing to YOU. Step outside your comfort zone. If an idea makes you feel like there are butterflies in your stomach, that's something you want to write down! Get a diary or journal and make notes of your thoughts and ideas. As you begin to achieve some of the goals, write about how you feel before, during, and after the adventure. Every time I've been to a foreign country I've kept a journal, and it's exciting to read over the details years later.

As you make a list, remember the things you loved to do when you were a child, like flying a kite, or going skinny-dipping. Maybe you enjoyed riding go-carts and you can re-experience that thrill, or find a NASCAR track where they will allow you to ride along, and maybe even drive a real racecar! March in a parade, sing karaoke, and walk on a beach at sunrise, and again at sunset. Go skydiving, visit all of the US National Parks, build a treehouse, see the Seven Wonders of the World, or view the Northern Lights. Watch a ball game with your grandchildren, or visit your best friend that you haven't seen in twenty years. Your ideas can be as magnanimous as going on an expedition to Antarctica, or as humble as writing a letter to a lonely man or woman serving in the military.

If you've always wanted to travel, make plans to visit the locations that appeal to YOU, not necessarily the hot tourist spots. Check into the possibility of a "home exchange" where you swap homes with someone for a while. This is another concept made popular by a movie. *The Holiday* features two single women who swap their respective homes in England and California, and have great adventures. Airbnb is an economical option for lodging, as is Couch Surfing, although these unconventional options might not appeal to everyone.

What if you have a companion that has a different bucket list? Maybe you don't like each other's choices, or you aren't physically capable to join them on their quest. At the very least, make an attempt to share their excitement and joy. I find the idea of skydiving more frightening than fun, but if a friend wants to try it, I will be there to support them, waiting on the solid ground. On a trip to a theme park with my grandson, I vowed to ride all the roller coasters with him. The first one was smooth and fun, but the second ride was rough and bounced me around like a rag doll. I had to reconsider, and decided the rest of the day wouldn't be much fun if my grandson had to see me carted off in an ambulance. I did stay close and watched him as he enjoyed the rest of the coasters.

You might not be able to accomplish everything on your list due to health limitations or financial restrictions, but write them down anyway. Perhaps you can't climb Mount Everest, but you can live vicariously through someone else who has done it, or watch a documentary about the challenging feat. Traveling can be expensive and you might not be able to go to everyplace on your list, but you can read books and watch movies that take you on an armchair tour. My personal belief is, that we can always find a way to do the things we **really** want to do. It might take a few years to save enough money for the #1 item on your bucket list, but you can research and discover every minute detail about the adventure and look forward to the day you will fulfill your dream.

Remember, as you create and accomplish your very own bucket list, not everything has to be a spectacular challenge or expensive excursion. Often the little things in life end up being the most important. Think of the things that make you smile, thrill your soul and bring joy to your heart. That's what a bucket list is all about. "One day your life will flash before your eyes. Make sure it's worth watching"(Gerard Way).

Conclusion

I hope that the ideas I've presented in this book have been helpful in encouraging you to discover and pursue the things that make you happy in your retirement years. Start now, by writing your list of things to make it happen!

- Recognize what is most important in my life.
- Get my house in order and take care of the necessary documents for my family to follow my directives.
- Decide the best living situation for ME.
- Contemplate and plan adventures.
- Learn how to stay healthy and keep my mind active.
- Achieve the spirituality that I desire.
- Create my bucket list.
- Don't be afraid to dream a new dream each day.

Don't forget to check out the Resource section for more information and links to some of the ideas presented within the book. The best way to find out what's happening locally, and to research activities and adventures that appeal to you, is to get on the computer and search. Keep a notebook close by to write down ideas. You might add something new every day, or cross off items that you've reconsidered. Keep a daily journal to track your progress. It will be fun to read it later and see how far you've come!

Remember - There's no right or wrong! This is your journey and your time to create the retirement of your dreams. Don't be hesitant to explore different options to discover the many ways of fulfilling your vision and enjoying the life you deserve. I wish you joy and contentment as you discover what makes you happy, and leave you with some great advice. *Don't hesitate or talk about what you want to do. Just do it.* (Gbenga Akinnagbe)

Resources

The following information will clarify some of the ideas presented in the content of this book, and assist you as you research the things in YOUR life to bring you joy in your retirement years. At the time of publication, the links provided are active. The author endorses these resources for entertainment purposes, and is not associated or compensated by any business or service and makes no claim as to the content within a website.

This list is a sample of the ideas available to you, and there are hundreds more that you can find that will meet your specific needs. Look for local sites that relate to your specific location. Check your library for excellent resources, such as the "For Dummies" series that will help you learn just about anything.

Chapter 1

Dog sitting
Rover:
https://www.rover.com/become-a-sitter

Dogvacay:
https://dogvacay.com/how-it-works

Freelance Sites
UpWork:
https://www.upwork.com/i/howitworks/client

Guru:
http://www.guru.com/howitworks.aspx

Freelancer:
https://www.freelancer.com

Thumbtack:
https://www.thumbtack.com

Uber:
https://www.uber.com

Care Services
CareGivers:
http://www.caregivers.com

Care:
https://www.care.com

Sitter:
http://sitter.com

Chapter 2

Keeping Tax Records
https://www.irs.gov/Businesses/Small-Businesses-&-Self-Employed/How-long-should-I-keep-records

Local sell or swap sites
Ebay, Craigslist or Facebook

Decluttering
Spark Joy:
http://mostlovelythings.com/spark-joy-organizing

HGTV Tips:
http://www.hgtv.com/design/topics/decluttering

Zen Habits:
http://zenhabits.net/15-great-decluttering-tips

Becoming Minimalist:
http://www.becomingminimalist.com/creative-ways-to-declutter

Important Documents:
https://www.fdic.gov/news/conferences/affordable/hcachecklist.pdf

Chapter 3

Tiny Houses:
http://www.countryliving.com/home-design/g1887/tiny-house

Minimalist Living:
http://www.theminimalists.com

Chapter 4

Orient Express (Venice-Simplon):
http://www.belmond.com/venice-simplon-orient-express/luxury-trains

National Parks:
https://www.nps.gov/index.htm

Passport:
http://www.uspassportnow.com/passportapplicationservices

List of Senior Discounts:
https://onmogul.com/stories/this-list-of-senior-discounts-for-people-over-50-might-be-the-best-thing-you-learn-all-day

Chapter 5

Undiet:
http://bemorewithless.com/the-undiet

Butter vs. Margarine:
https://authoritynutrition.com/butter-vs-margarine

Portion control devices:
http://www.theportionplate.com

Chapter 6

Geocaching:
https://www.geocaching.com/play

7 Must Do Marathons:
http://running.competitor.com/2015/03/photos/7-must-5k-races-united-states_124113

Bubble Run:
http://www.bubblerun.com

Hot Chocolate Run:
https://www.hotchocolate15k.com

Rock 'n Roll Run:
http://www.runrocknroll.com

Color Run:
http://thecolorrun.com

Chapter 7

Board Games:
http://www.boardgamecentral.com/games

Card Games:
http://www.ranker.com/crowdranked-list/most-fun-card-games

Chapter 8

Learn to code:
http://websearch.about.com/od/h/g/http.htm

Trip Planning
TripAdvisor:
https://www.tripadvisor.com

Lonely Planet:
http://www.lonelyplanet.com

Airbnb:
https://www.airbnb.com

Movie Extras:
http://www.newfaces.com/movie-extras.php

Chapter 9

Religions of the World:
http://www.religionfacts.com

Pay it Forward:
http://thehalfwaypoint.net/2009/09/50-simple-ways-to-pay-it-forward

Random Acts of Kindness:
http://www.wikihow.com/Practice-Random-Acts-of-Kindness

Chapter 10

The Bucket List:
https://en.wikipedia.org/wiki/The_Bucket_List

The Holiday:
https://en.wikipedia.org/wiki/The_Holiday

101 Things to do before you die:
http://personalexcellence.co/blog/bucket-list-manifesto/

Write to a soldier:
http://soldiersangels.org/letter-writing-team.html

Seven Wonders:
http://geography.about.com/od/lists/a/sevenwonders.htm

Home Exchange:
https://www.homeexchange.com

Couch Surfing:
https://www.couchsurfing.com

Acknowledgments

With great thanks to my family and friends who have offered me encouragement and support in making my dream a reality.

Your belief in me has inspired me throughout this project and continues to lead me to strive for great things every day.

About the Author

Olivia Greenwell, a recently retired hotel front desk manager, is now pursuing her long-term personal goal of becoming a published author. Residing in Tampa, Florida she enjoys spending her days going for long walks with her little dog Sammy, discovering a new love for baking, working on her writing projects and spending time with her two grand children.

Olivia's favorite thing to do is watch the sunset from the beach while reflecting on the day just spent and making plans for the next day.

Olivia is busy following her dreams in a happy retirement.

CPSIA information can be obtained
at www.ICGtesting.com
Printed in the USA
LVOW13s1812101216
516719LV00007B/648/P